D0877395

THE
SOCIAL SECURITY

Success Guide

Hidden Secrets Revealed to Maximize
Your Retirement Benefits

CHARLIE STIVERS

with Christy Sparks

a Garden Value Publishing book

The Social Security Success Guide

Published by

Garden Value Publishing

© 2016 by Charles Stivers. All rights reserved.

Copyright © 2016 Charles Stivers

ISBN-13: 978-0-9970543-0-9

ISBN-10: 0-9970543-0-1

Library of Congress Control Number is available from Publisher

Garden Value Publishing

6140 S. Gun Club Rd. #K6-199

Aurora, CO 80016

www.GardenValuePub.com

TESTIMONIALS

The Social Security Success Guide is the essential tool for everyone entering the Social Security maze. As the former owner of a successful financial planning firm with over 30 years of experience, I wish I'd had this book as the resource for my clients at one of the most critical financial times of their lives. Charlie takes a very complex and sometimes fearful process of navigating your Social Security options and simplifies and leads you to the best solution to maximize your benefits. I highly recommend this book to everyone.

-Gary Barnes
www.GaryBarnesInternational.com

As my wife and I approach retirement in the next decade, we've begun to explore our Social Security options. The more research we do, the more confused we get. The Social Security Success Guide is the first resource that simplifies the complex system and clearly explains our options. Finally, we feel confident we will make the right decisions as we ride off into the sunset. Thanks Charlie!

-Ted Prodromou
www.TedProdromou.com

Very few people have taken the time or effort to understand how the SS system works and how we can derive the most benefit from it. Charlie Stivers has. We can all benefit from what he has learned since he shares that knowledge in this book. Who knew that SS can be a well-rounded, benefit-packed investment or financial vehicle? Charlie Stivers did and now we do too. Thanks Charlie!

-Jonathan Manske
www.JonathanManske.com

As a successful business leader for over 30 years, I look at one thing when I read a new non-fiction book. ROI-Return On Investment. Charlie's book has a very high ROI. I know it's going to literally save me thousands of dollars during my retirement years. He's written a clear, easy-to-understand, no mumble-jumble book about the black hole called Social Security and how smart retirees can benefit from his sage advice. I'm going to recommend it to all of my friends as they approach their 60's.

-Chasen Chess – *America's Marketing Maverick®*, Founder and CEO at Successful Lives Unlimited

I made the decision to file for Social Security benefits, but was afraid to do it on my own. I knew if I made a mistake it would have huge consequences. I felt I needed the help of someone I trusted. Charlie led me through the online application step by step and helped me complete it in one session. I left feeling relieved and confident that it was done correctly.

-A. Price, Realtor in Denver, CO

Wow, "The Social Security Survival Guide" by Charlie Stivers is a must read for anyone wanting to retire. It provides viewers with practical information that can be used to reduce your worries about retirement planning and give you confidence to retire happy.

**-Anne M. Sandoval
State Farm agent, Aurora, CO**

The Social Security Success Guide is a MUST read for anyone that is confused about Social Security Benefits (And, even those that THINK they know all they need to know about Social Security); how to apply for it, how to maximize your benefits and where to start! This book gets right to the point with very specific step by step instructions. There is no extra fluff like many other "how to guides". I only wish there were books as succinct as this one for everything we need help with!

-Nicole Scott
Insurance Advisor, Santa Clarita, CA

Who knew there were Social Security loopholes? This book was an easy-read, offering great information on the how's and when's of filing for Social Security benefits in order to get the biggest payout. This is a great gift for folks approaching retirement. You'd be doing them a big favor by gifting this book. Highly recommend it.

-Sabrina Risley
www.CertusNetwork.com

Finally, a simple and easy to read, step by step guide that leads new Social Security recipients through the maze of their enrollment. Charlie helps individuals navigate their options to maximize Social Security dollars for the rest of their lives. I highly recommend the Social Security Success Guide to anyone entering their retirement years.

-Kevin Knebl, CMEC
Int'l Speaker/Author/Trainer
Social Selling & Relationship Marketing Specialist
Joie de Vivre Coach™

IN MEMORY
of my dad, Joel Stivers.

It all started with a
responsible dad teaching
his young son about money.

TABLE OF CONTENTS

TABLE OF CONTENTS

Continued...

INTRODUCTION

Imagine, it is now the year 2033. You're in your 70's, well into your retirement years, enjoying the grandkids, traveling and planning a trip you've always dreamt of going on, taking dance classes with your spouse once a week, volunteering in your community, and you have time and income to do what you want, when you want.

Your monthly cash flow allows you to not only play and create memories, but to afford good health care coverage, quality foods, a safe car, a comfortable home, and cover your living expenses. That extra $2,109 monthly check you receive from Social Security, after using some of our techniques you learned in the Social Security Success Guide, is the difference between just having a standard living, where you are just covering your living expenses, to now being able to sustain the quality life you worked so hard to enjoy. Your personal economy is strong and stable.

Then, the US Government announces it is now $100 trillion in debt....

Will you be one to breathe a deep sigh of relief because you read this book and planned appropriately for your retirement years? Or, will you be living a financially stressed life, dependent on others, living with your son or daughter, or having to miss out on special things in life like spending time with your grandkids?

Read on, and join the few who practice these well-kept secrets to maximizing your Social Security retirement income benefits that are available to you, as guaranteed by Uncle Sam.

PREFACE

If you had $1 million, or even $500,000, would you ignore it? Would you become impatient, and take income or withdrawals out of that account without a plan? Would you spend it frivolously? That is how most Americans treat their Social Security retirement benefit. According to SSA statistics, there are approximately 60 percent of retirees taking early retirement (ages 62-65) from Social Security—many without a plan.

There are a handful of reasons why and these are the top three I hear: we are ready to retire now and we want our money, (no patience), we think Social Security is too complicated (won't take time to understand it), and we don't think our benefit will be there if we delay (no faith in our entitlement system or government). Those are all valid reasons and are really lessons to be learned in human behavior, our social system and Americans as a society. Read further to see how this book will change your thinking regarding your Social Security retirement benefit.

This book has been written as a guide to easily educate future Social Security retirement income recipients on the best strategic income options available so they are empowered to make the best decisions for their family and themselves.

Along with providing the current seven best filing strategies for retirement, there will be specific life scenarios covered—for divorcees, widowers, and survivors. There will be general information regarding taxation, history, definitions, tables, and links. Some of these strategies will be phased out over time due to recent legislature for filers after April 29th, 2016, which is intended for the greater benefit of Social Security as an entitlement system for everyone. Caveats will be mentioned in areas that are currently in the process of being changed.

And, finally, you have a step-by-step tool to use to help you apply and file for your own benefit with confidence, so you do not have to go down to the Social Security office. This part of the guide has been some of my clients' favorite part in working with me. They love not having to go down to the administration office and that they can now file online in the comfort of their own home or at my office.

I think we all can agree that Social Security is a very complex subject. However, few of us are aware that Social Security retirement income planning has seven strategies and 81 different age combinations to consider (approximately 567 sets of calculations) when determining *how* and *when* to apply for your Social Security benefits. That's a whole lot of options that this guide will reveal and simplify for you!

To add to the challenge of deciding what to do and when to do it, is the fact that most Social Security recipients are dealing directly with Social Security Administration claims' representatives who have been in their positions less than three years, which makes them trainees by industry standard.

Good luck getting anything more than general information to your questions, as these representatives are instructed to give you only generic information. So, even if they could, they certainly wouldn't give you any advice. My experience is they make it easy and "suggest" to filers—take your money now.

Yes, to say it can be frustrating is an understatement. I hear it all the time.

This book is specifically designed to be your go-to guide when navigating and applying your earned Social Security retirement benefits. When you are ready to pull your hair out from getting the runaround, this guide will help you file (actually, show you step-by-step *how* to file) your own benefit online, with or without the help of someone from the Social Security Administration.

If you are a seasoned do-it-yourselfer—like many of us—my first suggestion is that you take the time to consult with an experienced retirement specialist and/or tax advisor to develop a retirement income strategy based on your personal needs and goals before you make any kind of choices concerning your selection.

It becomes more and more apparent why I say this for reasons that we will build upon throughout this quick and valuable guide.

My second suggestion is that you register on the Social Security Administration website at www.socialsecurity.gov (or www.ssa.gov) even if you are a several years away from receiving Social

Security. For all the retirement related links in one page go to:

http://www.socialsecurity.gov/planners/retire/
or: http://1.usa.gov/1OkatvW

Registering on the www.ssa.gov website is simple, but occasionally I hear that some people cannot find a match of their record online, or they ran into some kind of glitch. It is better to find out now if you have errors so you have the most time to get them corrected. Worst case scenario is that you have to go to your regional Social Security office or call in to make an appointment. Don't get frustrated, the appointments over the phone are effective and productive. Just for your information, the regional offices and service representatives are typically booked 30 to 60 days out for appointments and it's crowded all the time with 100-200 people.

Once you are at the website, go to the "my Social Security" tab and register for your own account. Again, I'll walk you through it step-by-step in the first section.

How to Get the Most Out of the Social Security Success Guide

Use this guide as you would a resource or reference book. Make notes in the margins, highlight key points, star and underline, and/or dog-ear the pages, like you would in a work book. If you need a "clean" copy, you can always contact me, and I'll be more than happy to provide a new one for you.

Secondly, I think we are going to see a lot of changes of to our entitlement programs like Social Security and Medicare.

Now go to: www.SocialSecuritySuccess.Guide

(Yes, there is a .guide for websites now in addition to .com or .gov.)
Subscribe to our list and stay informed about the latest news, updates and changes regarding these issues.

Bottom line is, the ssa.gov website has all the information you need to know, but do you know what information you are looking for? What questions you should be asking? Where do you find the right, specific information? I have enclosed direct links to the relevant information for your convenience throughout the chapters and again at the back of the book. For your convenience, I used bit.ly to shorten many of these links. There are plenty of hidden strategies that are available, but the ssa.gov website does not currently have a direct, clickable link to navigate from the home page—you have to know what you are searching for.

Ultimately, how you take in and process all that information as it applies to you and/or your spouse's financial situation is critical. You have to optimize what you have for Social Security benefits with your other income sources, assets and taxes to develop the best retirement strategy and income plan to last you for the rest of your life.

Simple, right? Not.

And, as a bonus, wouldn't it be nice to have more than enough to leave a legacy for your heirs to remember you by?

Here's some good news in all this…If you mess up your benefit selection the first time, you do get one chance for a "do over." Yes, you get one mulligan, redo, second-chance, provided you file again within the first 12 months of filing for Social Security. There are some catches with this that are addressed later in the book. But, then you only have one chance to get it done the right way for you. This last selection is going to be your starting point, no matter what, for the rest of your life! So, we really want to get it right the first time.

My Promise to You

My promise is to simplify Social Security income concepts and to help you make sense of the best strategies to optimize your Social Security income for your retirement. To put it even more simply, **I want to help you put more of your hard-earned tax dollars back in your pocket.**

I know *The Social Security Success Guide* can help you and your spouse not only survive the Social Security retirement income maze, but also thrive in your golden years with your Social Security retirement benefit as a foundation (or one leg) of your retirement income sources.

How I Came to Learn About Social Security Benefits

This little guide grew out of my experience in helping my mom, who was divorced and close to retirement, research and apply for benefits at the Social Security Administration office in Boulder, Colorado. We had a hard time understanding and making any sense of the government jargon and lack of instruction provided to us. Even though I had the aptitude of learning and applying all these financial concepts, we had to go back a second time for more accurate information. If I had known then what I know now, we calculated mom would have received an additional $40,000 over a 10-year period. I don't want that to happen to you.

Because of this experience, I became relentless and passionate about knowing all these tactics and strategies guaranteed to us by Uncle Sam. My interest in helping people directly with Social Security and retirement continued, and then I met Christy Sparks through my relationship with Gordon Marketing, my insurance brokerage.

Christy Sparks has been a resource, as well as an advisor to advisors for everything to do with annuities and Social Security. She was the perfect authority to share her expertise in writing this book. With her help, I developed and held educational seminars for pre-retirees and retirees on Social Security benefits and strategies, and I continue to do so on a monthly basis.

Through all of my research and passion for learning everything I could about Social Security, I saw a real need for a simple, understandable guide that anyone could finish on an airplane trip or over a few nights before bed time.

Don't Pay the Idiot Tax

I want you to use this book as a tool to educate yourself to design the Social Security income piece of your retirement income portfolio, because <u>after your first 12 months, there are no do-overs with Social Security.</u>

I strongly believe in doing it right the first time and helping people avoid, what I hear people say, "paying the stupid tax." Dave Ramsey has made this phrase popular so credit goes to him for that, although it appears it is not trademarked.

The difference between making the best decision and possible financial scenario for you and making the decision that creates the worst possible financial decision for you when you start your Social Security income can be more than $100,000. I don't want that person or family to be you.

We would love to hear from you. –Charlie

For more information, contact:

CHARLIE STIVERS

6140 S. Gun Club Rd. #K6-199
Aurora, CO 80016
303.875.4695
Work: charlie @ GardenFinance.com
Personal: cgstivers @ gmail.com

CHRISTY SPARKS

Gordon Marketing
20236 Hague Road
Noblesville, IN 46062
800-388-8342 x 374
Work: csparks @ GordonMarketing.com
Personal: christyl.sparks @ gmail.com

SUBSCRIBE:
www.SocialSecuritySuccess.Guide

ACRONYMS

Commonly used acronyms by advisors and
Social Security professionals:

SS –   Social Security

SSI –   Social Security Income (abbreviation only)

SSI –   Supplemental Security Income (real name)

SSDI –   Social Security Disability Income

SSA –   Social Security Administration

FRA –   Full Retirement Age

NRA –   Normal Retirement Age (same as FRA)

PIA –   Primary Insurance Amount

DRC –   Delayed Retirement Credits

WEP –   Windfall Elimination Provision

GPO –   Government Pension Offset

COLA – Cost of Living Adjustment

FICA –   Federal Insurance Contributions Act

If further clarification is needed:

SSI – Officially refers to the Supplemental Security Income entitlement program, which many refer to as SS(D)I or Social Security Disability Income. They are similar but slightly different.

SS – Mentioned throughout this book refers to Social Security for Retired Workers or Old Age and Survivors benefits (OASDI).

TEXTING CODES

Commonly used texting codes that we
thought you might find a little humor in.

ATD –	At the Doctors
FWIW –	Forgot Where I Was
GHFA –	Got Hot Flashes Again
GHBA –	Got Heartburn Again
CRS –	Can't Remember Sh*t
CHS –	Can't Hear Sh*t
TTYL –	Talk to You Louder
KAW –	Kids Are Watching
GKAW –	Grand Kids Are Watching
SHCOON –	Shooting Hot Coffee Out of My Nose

We love to have fun with these text codes and acronyms. If you see or hear any fun acronyms we missed, or don't know about, we would appreciate you sharing them on our Facebook page:

www.facebook.com/gardenfinancial

NOTES / ACTION ITEMS:

CHAPTER 1

THE GROUND RULES

Tips for maintaining simplicity, consistency
and clarity while reading this book.

RULE #1

Most of the strategies to optimize your income payments are not available until you reach Full Retirement Age (FRA).

RULE #2

For purposes of this book, we will use age 66 as FRA.

RULE #3

Rules and assumptions will apply to those born between 1943-1954.

RULE #4

Your income benefit is based on <u>your</u> age.

RULE #5

Spouses have two income benefit elections: their own or half of their spouse's.

RULE #6

For single filers with no survivor, divorcee, or spousal benefits, your best option (really your only option) is to wait as long as possible. Ideally, wait until age 70 and live life to the fullest!

RULE #7

No increased benefits for waiting past age 70.

CHAPTER 2

MY SOCIAL SECURITY ACCOUNT

For printable instructions in a pdf file
search: SSA publication number: **05-10540**

To register your account online go to:

www.ssa.gov/myaccount

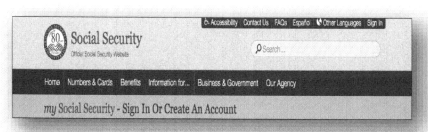

If for some reason the direct link has changed, go to www.ssa.gov and look for the "my Social Security account" tab or icon. There is no fee to register, but <u>you must have an email address.</u>

(If you don't have an email address, call a grandkid to help you. Otherwise, get on the Internet, go to www.gmail.com and follow the directions to set one up for yourself.)

Create your own personal account so you can verify and review your Social Security and Medicare benefits. You also will have an estimator that can calculate an approximate benefit based on your numbers that are disclosed in "Your Social Security Statement" at the top of page 2. We in the industry refer to this amount as your Primary Insurance Amount or PIA, which is coming up in Chapter 3.

Be sure to verify your mailing address, contact information and your direct deposit banking information. Another resource you have is the ability to print out a "Benefit Verification Letter", in case you need proof of income for applying for a mortgage, loan, etc.

STEP 1:

Select "Create an Account"

Get your free personal online *my* Social Security account today!

You probably plan to receive Social Security benefits someday. Maybe you already do. Either way, you'll want a *my* Social Security account to:

- Keep track of your earnings and verify them every year;
- Get an estimate of your future benefits if you are still working;
- Get a letter with proof of your benefits if you currently receive them; and
- Manage your benefits:
  - Change your address;
  - Start or change your direct deposit;
  - Get a replacement Medicare card; and
  - Get a replacement SSA-1099 or SSA-1042S for tax season.

Setting up an account is quick, secure, and easy. Join the millions and create an account now!

With instant access to yo   al Security Statement at any time, you will no longer receive one periodically   mail, saving money and the environment. Thank you for Going Green!

If you would like   ive your *Social Security Statement* by mail, please follow these instructions.

| Create an Account | Sign In | Enter Activation Code |

To create a "my Social Security" account you must: Be 18 years old, and have a valid email address, a Social Security number, and a U.S. mailing address.

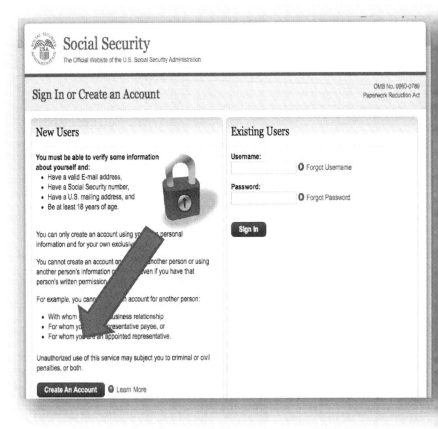

STEP 2:

Verify your identity by providing some personal information

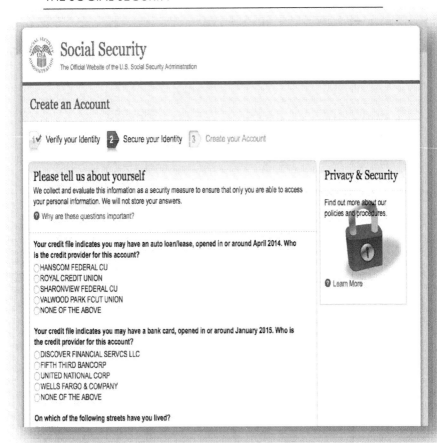

The Social Security Administration (SSA) pulls various financial records from your present and past to verify your identity. This can be the first step where potential records are mismatched and/or there is difficulty in recalling past history and financial accounts.

STEP 3:

Create your account details by choosing a username and password.

This process is as simple as creating logins for other websites. They guide you toward a strong password as well. Even the "forgot username" and password reset functions are easy to use, just as long as you remember the email you used to set up the account.

After you have created an account you will have access to your own annual statement. The next chapter walks you through your statement and what it all means.

CHAPTER 3

YOUR STATEMENT AND RECORD

To view your statement and record online go to: www.ssa.gov/myaccount.

Please read the first page of your statement, "What Social Security Means to You." Most importantly, start reading at the third sub-heading "About Social Security's future…" I always ask this question in my presentations and classes, "Who has read their statement starting on Page 1?"

Usually only 20 to 30% of class participants answer, "Yes."

If you are like most Americans, the only section everyone really reads or reviews is the one with the numbers that reflect their own work history of wages earned and the future benefits based on those numbers.

Online Social Security Statement

Estimated Benefits

About Your Estimated Benefits

- How you qualify for benefits...
- How we estimated your benefits...
- If you work in a job where you don't pay Social Security tax...

Retirement

You have earned enough credits to qualify for retirement benefits. At your current earnings rate, your estimated payment would be:

At full retirement age (66):	**$1,897 a month**
At age 70:	**$2,682 a month**
At your current age (65):	**$1,886 a month**

Your estimates are based on the assumption that you will earn $44,080 a year from now until retirement.

- Apply Online for Retirement

It is important to read your statement and stay informed about what is going on with your entitlement benefits and our entitlement programs, Social Security and Medicare. You are contributing to these entitlement programs our government has set up for all American workers and citizens, so don't you think it makes sense to pay attention to these real issues facing us?

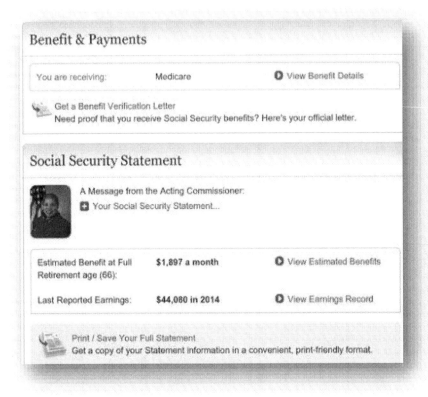

The following will break down what each page contains and the general message the government is informing you about and wanting you to pay attention to.

The included screen shots are meant for you to follow along and are not clearly legible. I encourage you to download and read your own statement.

The first page is basically a public service announcement and there is a warning to Americans that this is a very important entitlement program and "The Social Security system is facing serious financial problems" and "We need to resolve these issues soon to make sure Social Security continues to provide a foundation of protection for future generations."

They are also encouraging you to take personal responsibility for your own financial situation and future by directing you to go to **www.mymoney.gov** to learn the basics of financial management and personal finance.

When you get a chance, I recommend going to **www.myRA.gov** to learn about this new savings option set up by the Department of Treasury. I am hearing that regulatory authorities are pushing to require all financial advisors to inform and educate all their clients on this savings option.

Prevent identity theft—protect your Social Security number

Your Social Security Statement

www.socialsecurity.gov

Prepared especially for Wanda Worker

January 2, 2015

See inside for your personal information ➤

WANDA WORKER
456 ANYWHERE AVENUE
MAINTOWN, USA 11111-1111

What's inside…

What Social Security Means To You

This *Social Security Statement* can help you plan for your financial future. It provides estimates of your Social Security benefits under current law and updates your latest reported earnings.

Please read this *Statement* carefully. If you see a mistake, please let us know. That's important because your benefits will be based on our record of your lifetime earnings. We recommend you keep a copy of your *Statement* with your financial records.

Social Security is for people of all ages…
We're more than a retirement program. Social Security also can provide benefits if you become disabled and help support your family after you die.

Work to build a secure future…
Social Security is the largest source of income for most elderly Americans today, but Social Security was never intended to be your only source of income when you retire. You also will need other savings, investments, pensions or retirement accounts to make sure you have enough money to live comfortably when you retire.

Saving and investing wisely are important not only for you and your family, but for the entire country. If you want to learn more about how and why to save, you should visit *www.mymoney.gov*, a federal government website dedicated to teaching all Americans the basics of financial management.

About Social Security's future…
Social Security is a compact between generations. Since 1935, America has kept the promise of

security for its workers and their families. Now, however, the Social Security system is facing serious financial problems, and action is needed soon to make sure the system will be sound when today's younger workers are ready for retirement.

Without changes, in 2033 the Social Security Trust Fund will be able to pay only about 77 cents for each dollar of scheduled benefits.* We need to resolve these issues soon to make sure Social Security continues to provide a foundation of protection for future generations.

Social Security on the Net…
Visit *www.socialsecurity.gov* on the Internet to learn more about Social Security. You can read publications, including *When To Start Receiving Retirement Benefits*; use our Retirement Estimator to obtain immediate and personalized estimates of future benefits; and when you're ready to apply for benefits, use our improved online application— It's so easy!

Carolyn W. Colvin

Carolyn W. Colvin
Acting Commissioner

* These estimates are based on the intermediate assumptions from the Social Security Trustees' Annual Report to the Congress.

On Page 2 of your statement, it states "Your Estimated Benefits" for retirement, disability, family, survivors and Medicare. This is usually the first page everyone turns to, to read how big their benefits will be in the future. Here you will find a breakdown of your retirement benefits based on retiring at different ages. Again, it warns us these numbers are based on current law and to be aware that Congress can change them at any time. The very first number is the Primary Insurance Amount (PIA) you would receive at Full Retirement Age (FRA).

The bottom half of Page 2 talks about how a worker becomes eligible, and it gives you a link to the estimator tool with a **third warning** that the benefits may change due to changes in the law.

After stating this three times in one public, government-distributed document, you could probably deduce that this is some foreshadowing of times to come and you should be prepared for a worst-case scenario.

Then it states those estimates can be different based on the pension received from sources that did not pay into the social security system.

Windfall Elimination Provision (WEP) and Government Pension Offset (GPO) are the two different programs that are covered and explained regarding government retirement programs that are separate from Social Security retirement.

Your Estimated Benefits

*Retirement	You have earned enough credits to qualify for benefits. At your current earnings rate, if you continue working until...	
	your full retirement age (67 years), your payment would be about..	$ 1,702 a month
	age 70, your payment would be about	$ 2,121 a month
	age 62, your payment would be about	$ 1,174 a month
*Disability	You have earned enough credits to qualify for benefits. If you became disabled right now,	
	your payment would be about..	$ 1,544 a month
*Family	If you get retirement or disability benefits, your spouse and children also may qualify for benefits.	
*Survivors	You have earned enough credits for your family to receive survivors benefits. If you die this year, certain members of your family may qualify for the following benefits:	
	Your child..	$ 1,190 a month
	Your spouse who is caring for your child..	$ 1,190 a month
	Your spouse, if benefits start at full retirement age...	$ 1,587 a month
	Total family benefits cannot be more than	$ 2,941 a month
	Your spouse or minor child may be eligible for a special one-time death benefit of $255.	
Medicare	You have enough credits to qualify for Medicare at age 65. Even if you do not retire at age 65, be sure to contact Social Security three months before your 65th birthday to enroll in Medicare.	

* **Your estimated benefits are based on current law. Congress has made changes to the law in the past and can do so at any time. The law governing benefit amounts may change because, by 2033, the payroll taxes collected will be enough to pay only about 77 percent of scheduled benefits.**

We based your benefit estimates on these facts:

Your date of birth (please verify your name on page 1 and this date of birth)	April 5, 1975
Your estimated taxable earnings per year after 2015	$46,310
Your Social Security number (only the last four digits are shown to help prevent identity theft)........	XXX-XX-1234

How Your Benefits Are Estimated

To qualify for benefits, you earn "credits" through your work — up to four each year. This year, for example, you earn one credit for each $1,220 of wages or self-employment income. When you've earned $4,880, you've earned your four credits for the year. Most people need 40 credits, earned over their working lifetime, to receive retirement benefits. For disability and survivors benefits, young people need fewer credits to be eligible.

We checked your records to see whether you have earned enough credits to qualify for benefits. If you haven't earned enough yet to qualify for any type of benefit, we can't give you a benefit estimate now. If you continue to work, we'll give you an estimate when you do qualify.

What we assumed — If you have enough work credits, we estimated your benefit amounts using your average earnings over your working lifetime. For 2015 and later (up to retirement age), we assumed you'll continue to work and make about the same as you did in 2013 or 2014. We also included credits we assumed you earned last year and this year.

Generally, the older you are and the closer you are to retirement, the more accurate the retirement estimates will be because they are based on a longer work history with fewer uncertainties such as earnings fluctuations and future law changes. We encourage you to use our online Retirement Estimator at *www.socialsecurity.gov/estimator* to obtain immediate and personalized benefit estimates.

We can't provide your actual benefit amount until you apply for benefits. **And that amount may differ from the estimates stated above because:**

(1) Your earnings may increase or decrease in the future.
(2) After you start receiving benefits, they will be adjusted for cost-of-living increases.

(3) Your estimated benefits are based on current law. **The law governing benefit amounts may change.**
(4) Your benefit amount may be affected by **military service, railroad employment or pensions earned through work on which you did not pay Social Security tax.** Visit *www.socialsecurity.gov* to learn more.

Windfall Elimination Provision (WEP) — In the future, if you receive a pension from employment in which you do not pay Social Security taxes, such as some federal, state or local government work, some nonprofit organizations or foreign employment, and you also qualify for your own Social Security retirement or disability benefit, your Social Security benefit may be reduced, but not eliminated, by WEP. The amount of the reduction, if any, depends on your earnings and number of years in jobs in which you paid Social Security taxes, and the year you are age 62 or become disabled. For more information, please see *Windfall Elimination Provision* (Publication No. 05-10045) at *www.socialsecurity.gov/WEP.*

Government Pension Offset (GPO) — If you receive a pension based on federal, state or local government work in which you did not pay Social Security taxes and you qualify, now or in the future, for Social Security benefits as a current or former spouse, widow or widower, you are likely to be affected by GPO. If GPO applies, your Social Security benefit will be reduced by an amount equal to two-thirds of your government pension, and could be reduced to zero. Even if your benefit is reduced to zero, you will be eligible for Medicare at age 65 on your spouse's record. To learn more, please see *Government Pension Offset* (Publication No. 05-10007) at *www.socialsecurity.gov/GPO.*

On the third page, (the only page that <u>everyone</u> reads), it states "Your Earnings Record" that are your earnings subject to payroll taxes. It shows you how much you and your employer(s) paid in Social Security and Medicare taxes. You should confirm your earnings recorded here match with your records.

If you ever want to know the specific percentage of your income that you pay in taxes to your entitlement programs, it states that on this page as well.

An interesting point for high income earners is a portion of your income may go to Social Security up to a cap of $118,500 in 2015, but all of your earnings are subject to Medicare tax. It is likely that this will be an area that lawmakers will adjust to raise revenue for the Social Security trust fund.

On page four, it discusses "Some Facts About Social Security" in a basic summary for retirement, disability, family, and survivors. It also gives general information on what happens if you choose to take early retirement and links to their various publications on the subject.

Your Earnings Record

Years You Worked	Your Taxed Social Security Earnings	Your Taxed Medicare Earnings
1991	654	654
1992	1,651	1,651
1993	2,831	2,831
1994	4,759	4,759
1995	6,550	6,550
1996	8,238	8,238
1997	10,462	10,462
1998	13,676	13,676
1999	17,033	17,033
2000	20,174	20,174
2001	22,630	22,630
2002	24,652	24,652
2003	26,880	26,889
2004	29,593	29,593
2005	32,006	32,006
2006	34,682	34,682
2007	37,371	37,371
2008	39,173	39,173
2009	39,412	39,412
2010	41,344	41,344
2011	43,105	43,103
2012	45,140	45,140
2013	46,310	46,310
2014	Not yet recorded	

You and your family may be eligible for valuable benefits:

When you die, your family may be eligible to receive survivors benefits.

Social Security may help you if you become disabled—even at a young age.

A young person who has worked and paid Social Security taxes in as few as two years can be eligible for disability benefits.

Social Security credits you earn move with you from job to job throughout your career.

Total Social Security and Medicare taxes paid over your working career through the last year reported on the chart above:

Estimated taxes paid for Social Security:		Estimated taxes paid for Medicare:	
You paid:	$32,219	You paid:	$7,948
Your employers paid:	$33,984	Your employers paid:	$7,948

Note: Currently, you and your employer each pay a 6.2 percent Social Security tax on up to $118,500 of your earnings and a 1.45* percent Medicare tax on all your earnings. If you are self-employed, you pay the combined employee and employer amount, which is a 12.4 percent Social Security tax on up to $118,500 of your net earnings and a 2.9* percent Medicare tax on your entire net earnings.

*If you have earned income of more than $200,000 ($250,000 for married couples filing jointly), you must pay 0.9 percent more in Medicare taxes.

Help Us Keep Your Earnings Record Accurate

You, your employer and Social Security share responsibility for the accuracy of your earnings record. Since you began working, we recorded your reported earnings under your name and Social Security number. We have updated your record each time your employer (or you, if you're self-employed) reported your earnings.

Remember, it's your earnings, not the amount of taxes you paid or the number of credits you've earned, that determine your benefit amount. When we figure that amount, we base it on your average earnings over your lifetime. If our records are wrong, you may not receive all the benefits to which you're entitled.

Review this chart carefully using your own records to make sure our information is correct and that we've recorded each year you worked. You're the only person who can look at the earnings chart and know whether it is complete and correct.

Some or all of your earnings from last year may not be shown on your *Statement*. It could be that we still were processing last year's earnings reports when your *Statement* was prepared. Your complete earnings for last year will be shown on next year's *Statement*. **Note:** If you worked for more than one employer during any year, or if you had both earnings and self-employment income, we combined your earnings for the year.

There's a limit on the amount of earnings on which you pay Social Security taxes each year. The limit increases yearly. Earnings above the limit will not appear on your earnings chart as Social Security earnings. (For Medicare taxes, the maximum earnings amount began rising in 1991. Since 1994, all of your earnings are taxed for Medicare.)

Call us right away at **1-800-772-1213** (7 a.m.–7 p.m. your local time) if any earnings for years **before last year** are shown incorrectly. Please have your W-2 or tax return for those years available. (If you live outside the U.S., follow the directions at the bottom of page 4.)

The other take away is, it discusses Medicare and the basic coverages it provides. Then they warn us that, "Medicare <u>does not</u> pay for long term care, so you may want to consider other options like private [Long Term Care] insurance." <u>This is a key point</u>.

Again, the government is encouraging you to take responsibility and plan for your future.

Currently, there are only a handful of long term care options available on the market. Future health care costs are uncertain and hard to plan from the insurance companies' risk assessment point of view.

Many long-term care insurers have gotten out of that specific niche in the business. However, there are options in a select few insurance contracts that allow multiple coverages for the same premium.

This is not a sales book, so if you would like more information on long-term care coverage, please use our contact information at the beginning of the book to request more information.

If you need additional information or help from the SSA call 1-800-772-1213, or for the hearing impaired call 1-800-325-0778.

Some Facts About Social Security

About Social Security and Medicare...

Social Security pays retirement, disability, family and survivors benefits. Medicare, a separate program run by the Centers for Medicare & Medicaid Services, helps pay for inpatient hospital care, nursing care, doctors' fees, drugs, and other medical services and supplies to people age 65 and older, as well as to people who have been receiving Social Security disability benefits for two years or more. Medicare does not pay for long-term care, so you may want to consider options for private insurance. Your Social Security covered earnings qualify you for both programs. For more information about Medicare, visit *www.medicare.gov* or call 1-800-633-4227 (TTY 1-877-486-2048 if you are deaf or hard of hearing).

Retirement — If you were born before 1938, your full retirement age is 65. Because of a 1983 change in the law, the full retirement age will increase gradually to 67 for people born in 1960 and later.

Some people retire before their full retirement age. You can retire as early as 62 and take benefits at a reduced rate. If you work after your full retirement age, you can receive higher benefits because of additional earnings and credits for delayed retirement.

Disability — If you become disabled before full retirement age, you can receive disability benefits after six months if you have:

— enough credits from earnings (depending on your age, you must have earned six to 20 of your credits in the three to 10 years before you became disabled); and

— a physical or mental impairment that's expected to prevent you from doing "substantial" work for a year or more *or* result in death.

If you are filing for disability benefits, please let us know if you are on active military duty or are a recently discharged veteran, so that we can handle your claim more quickly.

Family — If you're eligible for disability or retirement benefits, your current or divorced spouse, minor children or adult children disabled before age 22 also may receive benefits. Each may qualify for up to about 50 percent of your benefit amount.

Survivors — When you die, certain members of your family may be eligible for benefits:

— your spouse age 60 or older (50 or older if disabled, or any age if caring for your children younger than age 16); and

— your children if unmarried and younger than age 18, still in school and younger than 19 years old, or adult children disabled before age 22.

If you are divorced, your ex-spouse could be eligible for a widow's or widower's benefit on your record when you die.

Extra Help with Medicare — If you know someone who is on Medicare and has limited income and resources, extra help is available for prescription drug costs. The extra help can help pay the monthly premiums, annual deductibles and prescription co-payments. To learn more or to apply, visit *www.socialsecurity.gov* or call 1-800-772-1213 (TTY 1-800-325-0778).

Receive benefits and still work...

You can work and still get retirement or survivors benefits. If you're younger than your full retirement age, there are limits on how much you can earn without affecting your benefit amount. When you apply for benefits, we'll tell you what the limits are and whether work would affect your monthly benefits. When you reach full retirement age, the earnings limits no longer apply.

Before you decide to retire...

Carefully consider the advantages and disadvantages of early retirement. If you choose to receive benefits before you reach full retirement age, your monthly benefits will be reduced.

To help you decide the best time to retire, we offer a free publication, *When To Start Receiving Retirement Benefits* (Publication No. 05-10147), that identifies the many factors you should consider before applying. Most people can receive an estimate of their benefit based on their actual Social Security earnings record by going to *www.socialsecurity.gov/estimator*. You also can calculate future retirement benefits by using the Social Security Benefit Calculators at *www.socialsecurity.gov*.

Other helpful free publications include:
— *Retirement Benefits* (No. 05-10035)
— *Understanding The Benefits* (No. 05-10024)
— *Your Retirement Benefit: How It Is Figured* (No. 05-10070)
— *Windfall Elimination Provision* (No. 05-10045)
— *Government Pension Offset* (No. 05-10007)
— *Identity Theft And Your Social Security Number* (No. 05-10064)

We also have other leaflets and fact sheets with information about specific topics such as military service, self-employment or foreign employment. You can request Social Security publications at our website, *www.socialsecurity.gov*, or by calling us at 1-800-772-1213. Our website has a list of frequently asked questions that may answer questions you have. We have easy-to-use online applications for benefits that can save you a telephone call or a trip to a field office.

You may also qualify for government benefits outside of Social Security. For more information on these benefits, visit *www.govbenefits.gov*.

If you need more information—Contact any Social Security office, or call us toll-free at 1-800-772-1213. (If you are

CHAPTER 4

QUALIFYING

To qualify for SS retirement benefits or to be considered <u>eligible</u>, you must be at least 62 and fully insured (meaning you have accumulated the required number of Social Security credits or some people refer to them as quarters).

An <u>entitled</u> worker is one who has applied for benefits (whether or not they are receiving them or have their benefits suspended). For eligible workers, that means that you need 40 credits or approximately ten years of work, which allows you to earn a maximum of four credits per year. Over the years the way you earn credits has changed, and in 2015, one credit is recorded for every $1,220 earned with a maximum of four credits per year.

Once you have at least 40 credits, the Social Security Administration (SSA) will calculate your benefits by looking at all the years you have worked and contributed to the system.

To simplify the calculation, the SSA averages the highest 35 years of earnings to calculate your Primary Insurance Amount (PIA). Your PIA is the full amount you would receive at your Full Retirement Age (FRA).

Determining your FRA depends on the year you were born. For people born before 1943, your FRA is 65. For people born between 1943 and 1954, the FRA is 66, and for those born after 1955, the FRA increases by two months every year until you reach age 67.

Determining
Your Full Retirement Age (FRA)

YEAR OF BIRTH	FRA
1942 or earlier	65
1943 – 1954	66
1955	66 and 2 months
1956	66 and 4 months
1957	66 and 6 months
1958	66 and 8 months
1959	66 and 10 months
1960 and later	67

DID YOU KNOW?

- ✓ The maximum monthly payment for 2015 is $2,663
- ✓ The average monthly payout for 2014 was $1,328
- ✓ By delaying your SS past 66 you get 8% growth per year on your income benefit

CHAPTER 5

WHEN TO FILE
VS.
HOW MUCH

The #1 Question I am always asked is, "When should I file for my benefits?"

The real answer always comes down to, "How much do you and your spouse need to live on?" The first question I always ask is, "What are your goals?" Before meeting with any advisor, write down your goals and dreams; have your spouse write down their goals and dreams, too.

It's also important to write down your concerns for the future - your health and other scenarios that none of us like to think about, but could happen at any moment. Ask yourself questions that start with, "What do I or we want to happen if…?"

If…even one of you experiences the unexpected in your life, then your whole retirement plan could be at risk.

After that, you and your spouse need to sit down with your financial and tax advisor to determine all income sources, assets, and estimated income taxes. Come up with a monthly and yearly budget.

The hope is that your goals don't exceed your budget.

As a general rule of thumb, most retirees plan on living on 70-80% of the income they were making during their earning years. Remember, when you turn 65, Medicare benefits start, and there can be some decent savings if you are healthy.

Maybe your home is paid off, too.

Based on this analysis, you should have a positive cash flow that you are comfortable with for retirement living. I advise my clients to continue to save discretionary income because it is a great habit, and keep a savings account because there are always unforeseen emergencies.

Six to 12 month's living expenses of liquid and safe capital or assets seems to be most retirees' comfort level. However, every person and every family is different. There are always many things in determining *when to file* vs. *how much.*

SHOULD I DELAY?

The first strategy I'll briefly touch on here and cover more in depth later, is to increase your Social Security income by waiting to take it. One of our partners in Social Security, the United States government, wants to incentivize each of us to delay taking Social Security income until age 70.

"Why?" you may ask.

First, they hope you work longer and contribute more to the Social Security coffers.

Second, the whole concept of "Time Value of Money" works great with large numbers and additional time for those huge numbers to compound. There is a reason why Albert Einstein is credited with calling compound interest the 8th wonder of the world or the greatest power in the universe. It sounds like something Einstein would say, but I cannot verify that anywhere legitimately.

And third, there is a chance that you or your spouse might die before taking benefits. Ouch!

The following table displays how your income payments are determined from taking benefits at age 62 to 70.

	Age 62	Age 66	GROWTH	Age 70
% of PIA	75%	100%	8% DRC	132%
Monthly Earnings	$750	$1,000	(+COLA)	$1,320

$1,000 represents the Primary Insurance Amount (PIA) at Full Retirement Age (FRA). This is the amount you would look for on your annual SS statement. At age 62, income benefits become available at approximately 25% reduction. DRC – Delayed Retirement Credits of 8% per year added to your benefit for waiting.

*NOTE: COLA increases vary and are not factored into the above calculations. Actual payments would be different and most likely higher over a four-year period.

SOCIAL SECURITY IS WORTH HOW MUCH?!?

Another way to relate how valuable your SS income is, is to equate what lump sum of money you would need to generate that guaranteed income stream from your portfolio. I will use round numbers and simple math using the same income benefit numbers of $750, $1,000, and $1,320 to illustrate my point.

PRINCIPAL	INTEREST		YEARLY	MONTHLY
$180,000	@ 5%	=	$ 9,000	$ 750
$240,000	@ 5%	=	$12,000	$1,000
$316,000	@ 5%	=	$15,840	$1,320

In my practice, I am starting to see PIA amounts of close to $2,000 a month for seemingly average yearly earnings history. So that can be equated to a lump sum value to that beneficiary of approximately $480,000.

Dual-income earners making higher wages are also becoming more of a norm. A household, or both spouses, receiving a combined $4,000 a month would equate to a $960,000 retirement account. This was a huge "ah-ha" moment for me one day when I was teaching withdrawal concepts to a client, and hopefully it is for you too while you are reading this book. I don't know about you, but it makes me think how valuable our Social Security retirement benefit really is to Americans, and how impactful it is to our financial plan in retirement.

Keep in mind, the added benefits of COLA increases every year and they are guaranteed by the government. These additional COLA increases are really there to keep pace with inflation and offset the increases in your Medicare premiums. There are no investments, annuities or savings accounts that offer all these benefits in a single contract. Again, this is a powerful way to look at how valuable the Social Security retirement system is to our retirees.

DID YOU KNOW?

By law, rules and regulations, there are only three entities that can "guarantee" your money, principal or interest rates.

✓ The U.S. Government

✓ FDIC Banks – backed by the U.S. Government up to account limits

✓ Insurance companies – Based on insurance company assets held in reserves regulated by <u>state</u> laws. (Also backed by state government up to account limits.) It is unethical for an advisor to sell or recommend an annuity based on the state guarantees. The state is merely a fail-safe if the company goes out of business.

Typically, the insurance companies that have found themselves on financially shaky ground in the past are companies with exposure to multiple lines of insurance in areas of: health-related insurance, accident insurance, and exotic types of insurance where the law of large numbers (which insurance companies rely upon) are limited. These are small niche-types of insurance companies of which usually no one has heard of.

The best way to protect yourself is to do business with highly-rated companies and to follow the rule of thumb: If it seems too good to be true, it probably is a sign of potential trouble ahead.

In an effort to meet the ever-changing needs of the market and policy holders, insurance carriers have become very competitive and more and more innovative with the features and benefits they are providing. Gone are the days of only being able to pick a separate, plain vanilla whole life insurance, and a separate long-term care or disability insurance plan that is "use-it-or-lose-it".

Now, they are adding features like income-doublers if the policy holder is confined to a nursing home. Or, they can advance the death benefit if the policy holder is diagnosed with a terminal illness, mental illness, chronic illness or critical illness. For example, there is additional coverage for heart attack, cancer or stroke victims who survive and need access to cash because they and their care-taker are not able to work.

Some of these insurance policies are solving the affordability problem of paying for life insurance, long term care, disability, living with cancer, or undergoing an extended treatment plan for a disease or injury. You have options of buying an all-inclusive type of policy. If there is a claim for one of these cases, then the insurance company makes an offer for the claim or advances the death benefit proceeds. Do not expect to have much of an additional benefit on top of the original claim if it is major.

This is a perfect example of how an experienced and well-informed advisor can help you find the best solutions for your long-term retirement planning needs—so you and your spouse can enjoy your golden years with peace of mind. Our office has resources and access to these types of policies—if you need help or you do not feel your current advisor has access to or is not aware of these types of plans.

LONGEVITY

What does your family's history of longevity look like? It doesn't always work this way, but a family's history of longevity, and your own personal health, may show you the best indication of how long you could potentially live. As a general rule, if you are healthy and you think you have a chance of living at least into your 80's, you should wait until your Full Retirement Age (FRA), at the earliest, to take your income benefit. You may want to consult your doctor and really evaluate this with him or her. Do your part and get your health checked; get those big exams done that you know you should have had tested 10 years ago. Put together a wellness plan— regular exercise, a balanced diet, and regular medical check-ups. There are many books and other advice on that subject, but start somewhere and make your health a priority for you and the ones who love you.

There is no greater, damaging blow to your financial wellness than bad physical health or chronic sickness, especially in your early years of retirement. So again, take care of yourself! Hopefully, it's not too late to take personal responsibility for your health. Involve your spouse and make it fun to get healthy together.

KEY POINT

✓ If you read the last page of your Social Security Statement it says, "Medicare does not pay for Long Term Care…"

WAKE UP!!

A final point about when to take your Social Security income. This is <u>YOUR</u> financial wake-up-call and my advice. Social Security was originally designed to be one of three main sources of income—pension, retirement savings, and Social Security.

Today, that still holds true except pensions have been replaced by 401(k)'s for the majority of retirees.

Retirement Income

1. Personal Savings
2. Social Security
3. Retirement Benefits
4. Part-Time Employment (Optional)

Do you think, or know, you haven't saved enough for retirement? Or, are your finances a total mess and riddled with bad habits? Do you know you will be dependent upon your Social Security income for a majority of your retirement income? All hope is not lost then, but most likely you and/or your spouse need to face reality—keep working and earning an income.

If you don't get your finances in order, you will be adding a fourth leg to this stool permanently or until you cannot physically work any longer. It is in your best interest to keep building your financial house, improve your financial habits, stick to your budget, pay down your debts, establish higher earning years that get credited to the Social Security income calculation, and delay your SS income so your DRCs grow as much as possible. Once one of you turns FRA, you now have options that we will address later in the book.

WHAT'S THE BREAK-EVEN POINT?

Charlie's gratuitous disclaimer

Come back to this part later if math hurts your brain like it can mine after a long day. Move on to Chapter 6, but come back to this point because it's interesting to look at how the numbers work.

If you are curious, the rough math calculations on the break-even point between early income benefits versus delaying to a larger income amount is approximately 12 years. I'll get back to that in a moment.

First check out this interesting point about age 82 being the magic, break-even age. The timing from age 62 – 82 (20yrs), from age 66 – 82 (16yrs), or 70 – 82 (12yrs) all work out to roughly the same sum total of all monthly payouts, and the SSA designed it this way. The only variable factor is peoples' own mortality and COLA.

With mortality being the major, unknown variable, the potential recipient loses the gamble of waiting to take a higher SS income payment, but your surviving spouse may thank you for the rest of their life. We address this later in the Survivor Benefits chapter.

MAGIC AGE 82 EXAMPLE:

I'll show the math (with no COLA) two different ways using the same payout numbers $750, $1,000, and $1,320:

@70	$1,320 x 12mos x 12yrs = $190,080
@66	$1,000 x 12mos x 16yrs = $192,000
@62	$750 x 12mos x 20yrs = $180,000

Finally, here's my point about 12 years. Imagine taking income at age 62 because you want your money now. We'll continue with the same payout of $750/mo. to age 66.

66 – 62 = 4yrs
$750 x 12 x 4 = $36,000

Now you've waited four years, let's use your payment of $1,000/mo. to determine the rough breakeven point it takes to recoup waiting four years.

At 66 you will see an increase to $1,000.
$1,000 − 750 = $250
$36,000 / 250 = 144 months or 12 years

Now let's use your payment of $1320/mo. to determine the rough break-even point it takes to recoup waiting another 4 years.

70 − 66 = 4yrs
$1000 x 12 x 4 = $48,000

At 70 you will see an increase of 32%.

1320 − 1000 = $320
$48,000 / 320 = 150 months or 12.5 years

The simple math doesn't lie. If you are planning on, or hoping, to live past 82, it makes mathematical and financial sense to wait as close to 70 as possible.

At FRA, you and your spouse have some really great options that we will reveal in the strategies chapter.

CHAPTER 6

PENALTIES

If you wait until your FRA, you do not need to worry about penalties.

The SSA wants to incentivize you to wait until your FRA (age 66) or longer (up to age 70) to take your benefit. Or, to look at it negatively, the government is going to penalize you a few ways if you take it early at age 62. Depending on your income needs or projected life expectancy, you may want to or need to take early retirement. However, there are penalties for taking withdrawals prior to FRA.

Early Retirement Penalty

https://www.socialsecurity.gov/OACT/quickcalc/earlyretire.html

or: http://1.usa.gov/1NNZJXt

Early withdrawal penalties: 25-30% depending on your age, as previously stated. It decreases as you get closer to FRA. For a spousal benefit, it is a 30-35% reduction and if you want to switch to your own record in the future, the penalty carries forward to your own benefit.

In the introduction of the book I stated that roughly 60% of retirees take early retirement prior to age 66. Here are some more specific statistics for 2014:

For men:

Age 62   35.5%

Age 62 – 65   58.3%

For women:

Age 62   40.8%

Age 62 – 65   65%

Your Benefit Reduction for Early Retirement (age 62)

Year of Birth	Benefit Reduction
1943 – 1954	25.00%
1955	25.83%
1956	26.67%
1957	27.50%
1958	28.33%
1959	29.17%
1960 and later	30.00%

Spousal Benefit Reduction for Early Retirement (age 62)

Year of Birth	Benefit Reduction
1943 – 1954	30.00%
1955	30.83%
1956	31.67%
1957	32.50%
1958	33.33%
1959	34.17%
1960 and later	35.00%

Income Limit Penalty

https://www.socialsecurity.gov/OACT/COLA/
rtea.html

or: http://1.usa.gov/1Pmzry1

✓ Income limit restrictions or earnings' caps
that offset your SS income are based on
$15,720 for 2015.

For workers taking early SS retirement income,
there is an earnings' cap to keep track of if you want
to avoid a penalty. If you earn more than $15,720 in
2015, your benefit amount is reduced one dollar for
every two dollars you make over $15,720.

SOLUTION:

The best solution to avoiding a penalty is to
request suspension of your monthly SS check(s) for
the approximate amount of earnings over $15,720.

Your spouse's income is not included in the earnings' test.

The year you reach FRA, you are penalized one dollar for every three dollars you make over $41,880 up until the month you turn FRA.

KEY POINTS:

✓ The earnings' cap penalty is repaid back to you over time once you are over your FRA.
✓ If you are self-employed, they only count net earnings.

The benefits that are suspended or withheld for SS recipients who continue to work and find themselves subject to the earnings' cap penalty are not "lost".

I have not found an easy way to compute how they pay you back, just know that they do after you reach FRA. And those higher earning years can help give your monthly benefit a raise.

CHAPTER 7

"Closure of Unintended Loopholes"
Bi-Partisan Budget Act – Section 831

On November 2, 2015, Social Security became a bargaining chip in Congress to pass the newest budget deal and President Obama signed the new budget known as the Bipartisan Budget Act of 2015. Section 831 of the Act closes two key Social Security claiming strategies. Don't panic too much. It takes away added incentives for workers to wait to take their SS benefits. Lower earning divorcees will be hurt the most as I understand and apply it.

KEY INFORMATION:

- ✓ For anyone who is 62 or older as of 1/1/2016, there will be no changes to the deemed filing rule or to the restricted application strategy.

- ✓ For anyone who is turning 66 before 4/29/16 you should urgently determine if a File and Suspend strategy is best for your financial situation.

For everyone else who is younger than 62 as of 1/1/2016, there are two big changes:

DEEMED FILING RULES

Changed:

1. The deemed filing rule will be applicable to recipients 62-70 (previously 62 through 65). Even if you have reached FRA, if you file for retirement or spousal benefits you will be deemed to have filed for both types of benefits. You lose your choice and this **eliminates the Restricted Application strategy**.

2. Deemed filing applies immediately for any person when they become eligible for either spousal or retirement benefits if they're already collecting the other type of benefit.

To summarize what "deemed" means is, basically, SSA gives you the higher of the two, individual or spousal benefits, automatically.

SUSPENSION OF BENEFITS

File and Suspend, Lump Sum Strategy
Eliminated:

There will be three changes while your benefits are suspended:

1. You cannot receive a benefit based on anybody else's work record.

2. Nobody else can receive a benefit based on your work record.

3. There will no longer be the ability to retroactively un-suspend and receive your lump sum benefit.

These essentially eliminate the "file and suspend" strategies discussed further in the book if you are younger than 66 by, April 29th, 2016. And, to be clear, the new rules do not eliminate the ability to suspend, they change what happens while your benefits are suspended. You can still choose to suspend benefits if you change your mind. For example, if you file at age 64 and decide at age 68 that you wish you had waited, you still have the option to suspend benefits until age 70 and collect DRCs.

I labeled a CAVEAT clearly before all affected strategies in order to save you time in your reading and decision making.

WHAT TO DO NOW?

✓ If you are at FRA, you have until April 29th, 2016 to file and suspend your benefit and have your spouse or other family member claim spousal or other dependent benefits off of your record.

✓ The changes to the restricted application strategy and the deemed filing rule apply to anyone who does not turn 62 by the end of 2015. Individuals 62 or older are presumably not impacted by this change and, therefore, there is still an opportunity to still file a restricted application under this strategy once they turn FRA.

CHAPTER 8

STRATEGIES

Social Security filing strategies are actually not as complicated as they seem.

They are not about cheating the system or being sneaky or greedy. These strategies are the additional options the government has guaranteed us to utilize in order for us to maximize our benefits in our entitlement system. Think of it as a reward for waiting and incentive to keep Americans working longer. Well, Congress and our President just took away some of these incentives.

What we are starting to see now are the beginnings of some of these strategies starting to be eliminated. Unfortunately, some of these benefits are considered bargaining chips in budget negotiations in our Congress. These are the strategies available at the time of the writing of this book.

Subscribe on our website to be added to our list to receive the latest news regarding our entitlements and Social Security retirement benefits at:

www.SocialSecuritySuccess.Guide

What we don't know and understand often feels scary and intimidating. Remember, we are dealing with our government, and we all know there are secret or untold strategies that only the privileged few learn about. It is not taught openly by public institutions. It is up to us, Normal Nancy and Average Joe, to take personal responsibility to seek out and verify the information we need in order to make an educated decision.

The truth is—what you don't know can hurt you right in your retirement account. Read on and let us shed light on the seemingly daunting, scary shadows of Social Security filing strategies.

STRATEGY #1:

MAXIMIZING YOUR INDIVIDUAL BENEFIT

Delay Until 70 and Live Life to the Fullest

Let's start out by keeping this super-simple: Delay taking your Social Security income for as long as possible, up to age 70. There is no benefit to waiting past 70. I call this strategy, "Delay until 70 and live life to the fullest." In addition to the basic points and facts already given, here is another reason to delay taking your Social Security income:

Meet Normal Nancy. She has spent her income-earning years as a steelworker. As she grew to an executive level in her career, she traveled overseas much of the time for work and had little time to spend looking for a spouse. She worked very hard all those years and had stress and high blood pressure to prove it. She put the maximum amount possible into Social Security with all her paychecks, and now, at 62, she is ready to get her benefit and finally settle down with her 12 cats. Why not? She earned it! She has certainly worked hard enough and deserves her benefit as early as possible…right?

That may be true, but has she worked long enough and earned enough to enable her time to earn another 8% each year in interest as well? Nancy doesn't have to continue working in the steel business or any business for that matter if she chooses not to, but there may be more financial benefits for her waiting to take Social Security until all those Delayed Retirement Credits (DRCs) have paid off.

This scenario would be one for an advisor to step in and help her with, because she was a great saver and investor. If Nancy had a 401(k) from all those years of work or a pension plus other assets, there are smarter ways to take an income from those assets, allowing her SS benefit to grow in the meantime, and there are tax advantages to this approach as well.

KEY POINT:

✓ Your individual benefit is determined by your best 35 years of earnings as reported to the IRS.

For example, if you had two years of minimal earnings in your 35 years of earnings history, it may behoove you to work two more years at greater earnings to get a potentially higher calculation.

Maybe two of those 35 years were zero earnings. Knocking out two years of zero earnings in the 35-year average can make a difference. This is another reason to establish a "my Social Security Account" on the ssa.gov website and do some calculations using the calculators right there on the site.

www.ssa.gov/planners/benefitcalculators.htm
or: http://1.usa.gov/1YBqGrx

Continuing to work for higher earnings in your 36th and 37th year would replace the lower years of earnings. In other words, any additional working years with higher earnings can help your PIA if you already have 35 years of work and earnings history.

I am not going to explain the methods that the SSA uses to calculate your PIA because it is just technical stuff they use behind the scenes. Just know they basically take the average of your highest 35 years of earnings and adjust for inflation.

Waiting until 66 or your own FRA is smart for many reasons. Now you have additional higher earning years replacing lower earnings years; your income is 100% of your PIA and many more options come into play if you are married.

Waiting until age 70 is wise. Now you have eight percent growth of your PIA plus cost of living adjustment (COLA) per year. Let's just say you get two percent COLA increases per year for four years. Now you have roughly a 10 percent increase per year for four years. So many people overlook this point.

The break-even calculations mentioned earlier are only based on the increase guarantees and the DRC that the SSA incentivizes you with. In the long run, or if you or your spouse live a long time, this can make a huge difference in your monthly checks. This will help pay for the increases in Medicare over the years as well.

REMEMBER:

✓ The maximum monthly payouts:
   @62 - $2,025   @66 - $2,663   @70 - $3,501

STRATEGY #2:

WITHDRAWAL OF APPLICATION – PAYBACK

Fill out **Form SSA-521** or go to:

www.socialsecurity.gov/planners/retire/

withdrawal.html

or: http://1.usa.gov/1JxTXXZ

YOU screwed up! Oops! Second thoughts? Do you feel as if you should not have taken SS income early? You have one lifetime chance at a do-over within the first 12 months only. And you have to pay it back. If you take income prior to FRA and continue past 12 months, you are locked into your base calculation for the rest of your life.

The SSA's formal name is called the Application for Withdrawal and Refiling. You may hear others call it a SS Reset, Redo, Do-over, or the Free Loan Strategy. It got these names because prior to 2010, you could file a do-over once, at any time prior to age 70 as long as you could pay back all your payments in full with no interest due, hence the free-loan strategy.

Now you have only the first 12 months to initiate the do-over strategy. You can file for benefits as usual at any time you are 62 and older. Then your Withdrawal and Refiling application (Form SSA-521) must be requested within 12 months. You must pay back all income benefits you received and all spousal and ex-spousal benefits, if divorced. That is where this strategy gets tricky if that applies to your situation. Again, no interest is due, just the full amount of payments received. It is as if you never filed for an income benefit claim.

As a result, you are now a year older, plus you had use of monthly cash payments—interest-free. This is the "Free Loan Strategy" that was a great option that you could do up to age 70 for all the years you received income. For people who had a large windfall or inheritance, this was a great strategy.

After repaying the income back to Social Security, it is possible to receive a tax credit for negative Social Security. Please consult your tax advisor for proper advice regarding this strategy.

STRATEGY #3:

NO SPECIAL FILING

Meet Average Joe and Normal Nancy; they will be our sample couple as we work through the explanations and details of the filing strategies. Joe and Nancy are equally climbing the executive ranks within their company, where they met. They are both VPs of different divisions. They are both on the career path in life and decided to just work hard and play hard.

They choose to not have a family and have no pets. They were among the first to represent the name "DINKs" or Dual Income, No Kids. By having no kids, they saved and worked their way up to higher incomes with fat retirement accounts and plenty of money in their savings accounts. Joe and Nancy are also close in age, and when they both were 62 they decided to retire early and enjoy traveling and golfing together.

They both filed for their own benefit and received close to the same amounts. The point with this election is they have financial options and resources plus they may have medical reasons as well. Luckily, they don't need the money. They now have the choice to spend their money either from Social Security income or from their investments.

A FAVORITE DISTRIBUTION STRATEGY:

In this case, (this can be applied to others if there are financial assets) while their investments are doing great, they can start liquidating those accounts and save their Social Security income. When their investment accounts are dipping due to downward fluctuations in the markets, they can live on income from Social Security, savings and non-market correlated accounts.

QUALIFICATIONS:

Each person must be 62 years old and eligible to receive benefits.

Now, let's talk about spousal benefits. Waiting until at least one of you is FRA is the game changer, if Congress doesn't take that option away.

SPOUSAL BENEFITS

Another benefit of being married is that you have two choices for your Social Security income benefits. You have your own individual benefit or your spouse's, and the SSA lets you to take the higher of the two.

The remaining strategies are based on the options you have between you and your spouse and the timing of when to receive those benefits. As stated earlier, if at least one can wait until FRA, you have even more options. The following strategies can help retirees and their spouses make the most of their Social Security income benefits. These are also the strategies Congress is limiting access to and will be phasing out. I will label those ones specifically as applicable.

TWO QUALIFYING SPOUSES:

Option 1 – Individual Benefit

Each spouse collects their own individual benefit amount.

Option 2 – Spousal Benefit

The lower earning spouse may take up to 50% of the higher earning spouse.

KEY POINTS:

✓ Only one can take a spousal benefit if you are married. No double dipping!
✓ Taking a spousal benefit does not penalize the other spouse's benefit...not even an ex-spouse.
✓ In order to claim spousal benefits, you must be at least 62 years old.
✓ For a non-qualifying spouse, you must have been married for at least one year.

WARNING!

If you elect to receive a spousal benefit before you reach FRA, your individual and your spousal income benefit amount will be permanently reduced.

STRATEGY #4:

FILE AND SUSPEND
www.socialsecurity.gov/planners/retire/
suspend.html

or: http://1.usa.gov/1MyrPE5

CAVEAT – Going away April 29, 2016. If you are turning 66 or older prior to this, you need look at the following options for you and/or your spouse before this date.

Joe and Nancy have been married for 45 years and they are both 66 years old, making them both full retirement age.

Joe has worked for the same company his entire career as a mechanical engineer, and has built up a pension as well as enough credits to have a rather hefty Social Security benefit.

Nancy, in this story, was a different kind of engineer: a domestic engineer, a home maker. Her full time job included many hours of overtime, but none of her work counted toward Social Security credits, leaving her with no benefit.

In this rather "traditional" scenario, when determining how to maximize the household benefits we need to look at all the benefits available to this couple. There are actually two: Joe has a benefit and Nancy has access to a spousal benefit.

How do you maximize this spousal couple scenario?

Using the file and suspend strategy, this couple can receive the rewards of Delayed Retirement Credits (DRC), as well as the immediate access to a spousal benefit.

The higher income earner, Joe, should file because his wife Nancy will now have access to her spousal benefit. And, the spousal benefit amount does not have the option of DRCs as Joe's benefit does.

In other words, there is no reason to wait to take a spousal benefit. The most Nancy can receive between ages 66–70 is whatever spousal benefit she is eligible for at her FRA or age 66.

By Joe filing, he enables Nancy to access that monthly check, which will equate to 50% of his PIA benefit. However, he must not simply file, but also suspend his own benefit, enabling it to grow the additional 8% each year he delays taking it up to age 70.

Putting this picture together, the household will be bringing in an immediate monthly check at the highest possible amount available for Nancy, all the while Joe is allowing his to grow to its highest possible amount at his age 70.

QUALIFICATIONS:

To qualify for the "File and Suspend" strategy, one spouse must qualify for their own benefits and be at FRA or older, up to age 70. The other spouse must be at least 62 and they must have been married for at least one year.

This is similar to the restricted application strategy. Both spouses also have work histories and qualify as eligible. This strategy works best if there is a larger disparity of income and the spouse who earned less knows that the spousal benefit will be greater than their own.

The spouse with the higher PIA files and suspends at FRA. The other spouse files "Restricted" to get spousal benefit equal to 50% of PIA of the higher earning spouse.

The spousal benefit is reduced if taken prior to FRA. An additional penalty is incurred on your own benefit if taken prior to FRA. The main goal of this strategy is to begin a spousal benefit for one spouse. The other spouse will continue to get DRCs on their own benefit or they may decide to start receiving their benefit at any time between 66-70.

STRATEGY #5:

FILE RESTRICTED

(Spousal benefit only)

http://www.socialsecurity.gov/planners/re
tire/applying6.html#&a0=1

or: http://1.usa.gov/1ONtlUz

CAVEAT – Changing January 1st, 2016 if you are younger than 62.

In our next scenario we have a prime example of the "norm" in American culture today. Average Joe and Normal Nancy have both worked full-time careers outside their home and each earned the necessary credits to merit a Social Security benefit.

This couple has a total of four benefits to choose from as they look at the household picture. (We will build on these strategies in the next two sections so you can apply them to your situation.) They each have their own benefit and access to a spousal benefit. However, they are limited to receiving only two benefits at a time and a total of three over time as a household. How can two people have three

Social Security benefits? This next filing strategy is called Filing Restricted.

Let's see how this works for Joe and Nancy. Nancy is 66 and still enjoying her career; Joe also is 66 and working full time. They are both eligible for their full Social Security benefit, but neither one needs to take their benefit and are advised to delay taking it so they can benefit from the 8% DRC each year they delay to age 70.

Because they are both FRA there is no limit to how much they earn while still taking a Social Security benefit. Therefore, Joe decides to take his spousal benefit, which equates to 50% of Nancy's PIA, and restrict taking his own benefit until he is 70, allowing it to grow at 8% per year.

Since Joe is filing restricted, he is able to have a spousal benefit now and get the reward of DRCs later down the road, all the while Nancy is gaining 8% per year while she delays taking her benefit.

In short, this household has one spousal benefit immediately at FRA and two benefits growing with DRCs for later, totaling three benefits over the life of their election period.

QUALIFICATION:

To qualify for this strategy, you and your spouse must be married for at least one year. One spouse must be at least FRA and qualify for their own benefits. The other spouse must also qualify for their own benefit and have already filed or filed and suspended.

This strategy works best for working spouses who are both eligible or qualify and have a disparity in income. But, when they are ready to retire after having received DRCs and COLA increases, the lower income earner will have a choice of his/her own benefit or a spousal benefit, whichever is higher. The higher breadwinner must be FRA or older. After FRA, either or both spouses can continue to work or retire.

The purpose of this strategy is to maximize SS income for working couples who have reached FRA. In this strategy, the higher income earner can File and Suspend their benefit and let DRCs grow at 8% per year, up to 132% at age 70.

Then the other spouse can file for a spousal benefit or File Restricted, 50% of spouse's PIA, without affecting either their or their spouse's income benefit. Only one spouse can collect the spousal benefit.

This is a powerful strategy that most retirees are not aware of and could have a dramatic impact on a couples' income for the rest of either of their lives.

Then at age 70, a spouse can stay on the other's benefit if it is higher than their own individual benefit.

The result of this strategy is having a choice of the higher amount, either greater of their own individual benefit or the spousal benefit of 50%.

The long term result is 132% of PIA at FRA for life and the surviving spouse gets either 50% of the spouse's FRA or the 132% of their own earnings record.

Not a bad deal if you can wait that long!

STRATEGY #6:

COMBINATION STRATEGY
(File and Suspend - File Restricted)

CAVEAT – Eliminated April 29, 2016

This was a scenario I was beginning to see more and more interest in as we were educating pre-retirees. I think you will agree as to why.

Average Joe and Normal Nancy are more of the typical, modern American family. On the outside they seem to have the perfect life. They have two children and two dogs. They both work hard and make great salaries at their jobs. When it comes to money though, they feel as if they are spending it all on their family just to live a normal life.

The kids both grow up playing soccer and baseball. They are taking swimming and music lessons. The family vacation gets squeezed in once a year; they've visited Disneyland and Disneyworld. Joe and Nancy love their kids and spend most of their money on increasing the quality of life for the whole family.

However, they saw the value of their college degrees paying off so they decided that saving for college for their children was a priority. The most they saved for their retirement was maxing out their 401(k). They stayed out of debt, opened up 529 college savings plans, and contributed to their 401(k)s that had a match.

Flash forward to their late 50s. After having both children graduate college, they are relieved and proud of themselves and their children for finishing college and they feel it has to be easier financially from here going forward. Then one day they get a call from the youngest child asking if he can move back in and live in their basement. Their oldest calls and says she is getting married.

Joe and Nancy realize that they still have 20 years left to pay off their mortgage. They have a home equity line of credit (HELOC) because they had to fix up the house, plus they had additional expenses for college on top of that. They also have much more student loan debt than they ever thought they would. The kids are helping with their student loans a little, but that's a 20-year plan too.

Then one day the stock market begins to decline and the economy begins to slow. They see their retirement funds taking a 30% dive over the next year-and-a-half. Now they have the most adorable grandchild added to the family as well. They turn 60 and finally begin to wonder about their own quality of life in their retirement years. They realize that it is not feasible to retire early and 70 is going to be a stretch as well. A wake up call finally happens and they decide to get serious about retiring someday.

They feel overwhelmed and seek help. After reading books and learning all they can to become financially literate, they determine that financial planning is too overwhelming to do on their own. They interview several advisors they heard good things about and decide to hire a financial planner.

The financial planner puts them on track to meet their goals, and helps them feel like they have hope for the future and won't have to work the rest of their lives. They even see if they limit their risk in certain areas, keep saving, pay off debt, stay disciplined, and keep working until 70, they can enjoy a quality life in their golden years.

One of the areas they didn't see was how much of a positive impact Social Security retirement income will be in their future. When they turned 60 they each got a copy of their Social Security statement.

They knew they wouldn't be taking early retirement, however they saw how much working over the years had paid into their Social Security and were excited at the benefit they would receive at age 66. They discussed this as part of their financial plan with their advisor and what they didn't know was at 66, the lower income earner could take a spousal benefit equal to half of the other's PIA without affecting their own benefit. Wow!

Now they had a little more money they could use to finish paying off their debts from college and raising kids. Then at 70, they had a well-diversified and risk-adjusted plan, a significantly higher Social Security retirement income, and combined, they could count on both with almost 100% certainty that it would be there for the rest of their lives.

QUALIFICATION:

To qualify for this strategy, you and your spouse must be married for at least one year. One spouse must be at least FRA to file restricted and qualify for their own benefit. The other spouse must also qualify for their own benefit and have already filed and suspended to enable a spousal benefit. This does not work for divorcees.

This strategy works best for working spouses who are both eligible or qualify and have less of a disparity in income. After FRA, either or both spouses can continue to work or retire. The purpose of this strategy is to maximize SS income for working couples who have reached FRA. In this strategy, the higher income earner can "File and Suspend" his/her benefit and let DRCs grow at 8% per year up to 132% at age 70. Then the lower earning spouse can file for spousal benefits or "File Restricted", which entitles them to 50% of their spouse's PIA, without affecting either their or their spouse's income benefit.

This is a powerful strategy that most retirees are not aware of and could have a dramatic impact on a couples' income for the rest of either of their lives. Then at age 70 each spouse can receive their own benefit. The long term result is 132% of PIA at FRA for life and the other spouse gets 132% of their own record as well. And don't forget those COLA increases too. They can really add up.

Again, not a bad deal if you can wait that long!

STRATEGY #7:

FILE AND SUSPEND

(Retroactive Benefits - Lump Sum Benefit)

CAVEAT – Eliminated April 29, 2016

From Joe and Nancy's previous story, let's focus on FRA at 66 and all details of their story remain the same as the combined strategy. Now let's flash forward to 68 ½ and Joe and Nancy come across an investment opportunity that the advisor also agrees has a great potential of adding to their goals and would be a great fit to their overall plan.

They have a chance to buy a property in the mountains of Colorado below market value. It has positive cash flow and they see the amount of potential future rental income it will receive. They can enjoy time there with their family and also have an appreciating asset.

Most of their money is in retirement accounts. There is not enough in cash, non-retirement accounts and non-qualified funds. Their advisor suggests an option that could help them raise a little more capital. Since Joe filed and suspended, Joe has access to his benefit as a lump sum as a retroactive benefit. Meaning he can get a big check for all those years he did not receive income from the date he filed and suspended to today's date!

His PIA is $2,000 and he has 30 months that he has suspended. Now he has a lump sum of approximately $60,000 available to him. Wow! Again, something that Joe and Nancy never knew could be an option for their financial future.

QUALIFICATIONS:

To qualify for this strategy, you must qualify for your own benefits and be FRA or older—up to 70. This option would work for a single or married person.

The purpose of this strategy is to provide a lump-sum benefit between the ages of 66 - 70. It is retroactive to the date of filing and suspending, and if you delay the receipt of your benefits you can receive a lump-sum of all past deferred income benefits.

The catch here is there are now no DRCs provided if you request it prior to age 70. If income payments are reinstated as well, they will continue as if they were never suspended.

This strategy could come in handy in a few situations. Imagine you had a need for additional money any time after file and suspending — an investment opportunity, emergencies, etc. This is the key—you have to file and suspend. If you did not, you would only be accruing DRCs and COLA increases with no lump sum option, just a higher income benefit. You never know, so my advice would be at least "file and suspend" once you reach FRA.

CHAPTER 9

APPLY ONLINE

Step by Step Guide to Filing for Retirement
Benefits on the SSA.gov Website

You can now file on-line at https://www.ssa.gov in the comfort of your own home. Many of my clients have called me with hesitancy regarding applying online and screwing up. After reading this chapter and with the information you have learned in this book you will feel comfortable, confident and empowered to make a decision on when and how to file for your retirement benefits. You should apply online three months prior to the month you want your payments to start.

To help you and/or your advisor know what to expect when filing online, I captured screen shots of the online application process. With this being a once in a lifetime experience for recipients, it is nice to know how the electronic process of applying for Social Security benefits will be processed in the modern era.

Once you complete the online application the SSA should or will usually contact you within 48 hours. The feedback I have heard is SSA representatives have been very helpful. They just want to make sure everything is accurate and it was filled out the way you intended it to be. They discuss the timing of when you can expect to receive your first payment. They will also address any particular scenarios that are different from just filing for your own benefit.

Also, be prepared to have a discussion if there are any applicable reduced benefits on your record. They can help you clear up any misunderstandings and discrepancies.

You also have the opportunity to add comments for clarification in the "Remarks" section at the end of the application for anything that you want to make sure is clear and have addressed in the follow-up conversation. For example, restate the projected earnings for the current year of work and the last date of employment. Anything that seems out of the ordinary, make a note during the application process and add in the remarks section.

STEP 1:

Go to:

https://www.SSA.gov

If you have not already created a "my Social Security account" yet, look for the clickable links on the SSA home page and complete this first.

STEP 2:

Click on:

"Apply for Retirement"

STEP 3:

After you have completed your account registration and you have "Signed In" to your account, you should be able to access your statement.

On this page, if you have not done so yet, first click:

"Print / Save Your Full Statement"

Benefit & Payments

You are receiving: Medicare   ⊙ View Benefit Details

 Get a Benefit Verification Letter
Need proof that you receive Social Security benefits? Here's your official letter.

Social Security Statement

 A Message from the Acting Commissioner:
⊕ Your Social Security Statement...

Estimated Benefit at Full Retirement age (66):	**$1,897 a month**	⊙ View Estimated Benefits
Last Reported Earnings:	**$44,080 in 2014**	⊙ View Earnings Record

 Print / Save Your Full Statement
Get a copy of your Statement information in a convenient, print-friendly format.

Make note of how your full name appears on your statement. It should match your application's information.

STEP 4:

Click:
> "View Estimated Benefits"

Review any of the Estimated Benefits links on this page for accuracy on your record if you need to do so.

STEP 5:

Scroll down a little and click:
> "Apply Online for Retirement"

STEP 6:

Click:

"Start a New Application"

or

"Return to Saved Application Process"

If you have a re-entry number from a previously saved application, this is where you would enter it.

Apply Online for Retirement/Medicare Benefits

Getting Ready

Before you start your application, we recommend that you take a moment to prepare yourself by reviewing a few items:

1. Make sure you meet the requirements to apply online for Retirement/Medicare;
2. Gather all of the information you need to complete the application process.

Apply & Complete

Applying for Retirement/Medicare may take between **10 to 30 minutes** to complete depending on your situation. You can save your application as you go, so you can take a break at any time.

| Start a New Application | or | Return to Saved Application Process |

STEP 7:

Check the applicable button and click:

"Next"

Mark the first button if you, the SS beneficiary, are filling out the application. An experienced advisor can be there to assist with navigation and completion.

The second button should be checked if the beneficiary is blind or has a disability that would require someone else's assistance, which will be disclosed during the application process. They ask if you are blind or have poor vision twice.

The third button would be checked if an appointed legal representative is completing the application for the beneficiary.

Apply for Benefits

Who Is Completing This Application?

Tell us information about the person completing this application:

○ I am applying for myself.
○ I am helping someone who wants to apply for benefits and is with me.
○ I am helping someone who is not with me, and therefore cannot sign the application at this time.

Next   Previous

STEP 8:

Complete the page with accurate personal information and click:

"Next"

<u>Important Note:</u> Make sure your application matches your name on your statement.

Information About Applicant

Your Name:
Please provide the name as it appears on the most recent Social Security card.

First	Middle	Last	-- ∨ Suffix

Social Security Number (SSN):

[ ]

Date of Birth:

-- ∨		
Month	Day	Year

Gender:
○ Male ○ Female

Are you blind?
○ Yes ○ No

During the last 14 months, have you been unable to work because of illnesses, injuries or conditions that have lasted or are expected to last at least 12 months or can be expected to result in death? ❓ More Info
○ Yes ○ No

`Next`

STEP 9:

Continue to complete your personal information (obscured below) and click:

"Next" or "Previous"

The "Previous" button works great too and it saves your information as you go. You will start to see the completed sections with a green check mark. Only click "Save and Exit" if you get stuck.

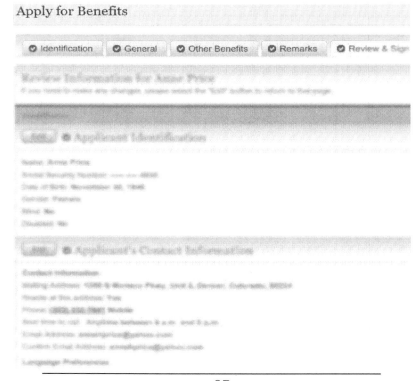

STEP 10:

Continue to complete the application in detail. It will ask you for some of the following information:

Marriage History, Work History, Earnings, Current Earnings (if working), Retirement Status or Projected Retirement

You will also have a "Remarks" section to add any notes or comments to your application. And you can ask to have a representative contact you.

Do not be afraid to hit the previous button if needed if there is a missing check mark on a previous tab. The system automatically saves the data as you click the "Next" or "Previous" button.

STEP 11:

Verify your information is complete and accurate and click:

"Review & Sign"

Then click:

"Print" and "Submit Now"

For pdf copies of screen shots go to:

www.SocialSecuritySuccess.Guide

CHAPTER 10

DIVORCEE BENEFITS

Joe and Nancy met freshman year of college in chemistry class. By the end of the semester they discovered that they had their own chemistry and began planning their wedding for the following spring. Joe continued his schooling while Nancy withdrew from school to dive into her role as a young wife. Nancy worked part time until they had their first child and by the time number three came along, Joe had finished his bachelor's and master's degrees.

The family moved many times to advance Joe's career. When he was finally at the top of his industry and their three children had finished college, Joe asked Nancy for a divorce. After giving her best income-earning years to her family and her husband, Nancy now found herself looking into her retirement years with anxiety in place of the excitement that she had always imagined.

She had not worked outside the home long enough to earn a Social Security benefit nor a pension or 401(k); she was completely financially dependent on her now ex-husband.

Thankfully, she was told by a financial advisor about the provisions that Social Security had put in place as a solution for people in just such a predicament. Divorce is a reality in American culture and leaves a lower earning spouse exposed to financial hardship throughout retirement. To stay true to its original purpose, Social Security had to adjust to protect and take care of those exposed to financial hurt because of divorce. The rules protect individuals like Nancy from being left with no benefit at all.

She will have access to Joe's spousal benefit just as if she were still married to him because she was married for more than 10 years and remained unmarried at the time she elected for Social Security. Thus, she was eligible for 50% of Joe's benefit.

QUALIFICATIONS:

If you and your ex-spouse have divorced, you may be entitled to spousal benefits if:
- ✓ You were married for at least 10 years
- ✓ You are both at least 62-years old
- ✓ You have not re-married
- ✓ 50% of former spouse's PIA must be greater than your own.
- ✓ **CAVEAT** - Divorced less than 2 years, ex-spouse must file and suspend by 4/29/2016

DID YOU KNOW?

- ✓ After claiming half your ex-spouse's benefit, you can remarry without affecting your current benefit amount.

You may be independently entitled without your ex-spouse being entitled if:
- ✓ Your ex-spouse is 62 or older
- ✓ The divorce has been final for at least two years
- ✓ Your own benefit would be less than 50% of your ex's PIA

CHAPTER 11

SURVIVOR BENEFITS

If your spouse or ex-spouse dies, Social Security provides benefits to the surviving spouse, which includes a small lump sum death benefit of $255. To apply for spousal benefits, a trip down to the SSA office will be necessary in most cases, especially if it is prior to FRA. There are a lot of different options and more rules in this case.

For example, survivor benefits are available at age 60 at a reduced amount (71-99%) until you reach FRA. Additionally, if you receive survivor benefits prior to FRA and keep working, you are subject to the yearly earnings limit and penalty. The earnings cap penalty will be in effect for the tax year, but it could be worth it to get additional, higher earning years on your own record. The penalty, if you are under FRA for the entire year, is a deduction of $1 from your benefit payment for every $2 you earn above the annual limit of $15,720.

As a widow/widower, you are eligible to collect a reduced amount of your deceased spouse's benefits at 60, or whichever is greater between you and your spouse's benefit if you are at least 62 years old. This means you can switch to the highest benefit at any time after 62. Here is the biggest benefit, potentially. While taking a survivor benefit at a reduced rate prior to FRA, you can switch to your benefit at FRA at an unreduced rate, if your benefit is higher. To simplify this, <u>there is no penalty to your own record for taking early income from your survivor benefit.</u>

Survivorship benefit rules are the most complex and vary depending on your situation. Call to make an appointment at your local SSA office ahead of time and invite your advisor to go with you since this could be an emotional time for you.

QUALIFICATION:

To qualify for survivor benefits you must have been married for at least nine months, or 10 years if divorced.

HINT: If you remarry after age 60, you are still entitled to receive spousal survivor benefits from your deceased former spouse.

CHAPTER 12

TAXABILITY OF SOCIAL SECURITY BENEFITS

"Who is this FICA guy, and why is he getting all my money?"
Rachel Green – "Friends" on NBC

There are many important choices to be made when considering not only Social Security elections, but also retirement income planning overall. It is sometimes said the number one fear in American is no longer death, it's: living too long and going broke! Americans are a hardworking, get-the-job-done type of people. We have worked hard for our families and our futures. The last thing we want to do is hand too much of our hard-earned money over to our long lost "Uncle Sam" or our cousin "FICA."

Anyone can maximize their SS benefits using the strategies in the book, but now with the taxation part of the equation entered into retirement, there is more to evaluate. Now we must optimize your plan for your specific goals, timing and strategies. This, again, is where proper planning and/or the right advisor can help you keep more of your income and your money.

Taxes are a topic that seem to strike fear in the minds of Americans; most are open to paying their fair share, just not too much. Some have the political view of—paying more in taxes makes sense if they benefit from it somehow in the future and if it benefits the American people as a whole. I greatly simplified that taxation tug of war, but finding that balance between the two sides is a constant debate.

We want to encourage you to flip on the light, look under the bed—really in the file cabinet—and see that there is no scary tax monster hiding there. We will debunk any misconceptions about your Social Security benefit and the taxes that you may have to pay. In the interest of simplicity, we will keep this conceptual and not dig into the details of the formula.

The formula is somewhat simple, and in the hands of an educated advisor or retiree there are many ways to protect yourself, your assets and the amount of taxes you would possibly be required to pay. You just need a strategy and a plan to keep yourself from over-paying the IRS.

According to the SSA, about 40% of current beneficiaries pay taxes on their Social Security benefits. If your income exceeds certain annual limits, a percentage of your Social Security benefits will be taxed. This happens if you have substantial income, including wages, dividends, interest, and other taxable income in addition to your Social Security benefits. What many of you will find interesting is what the IRS considers to be substantial income. The combined income formula is based on your adjusted gross income (AGI) plus any tax-exempt interest, which could be interest from municipal bonds and savings bonds, plus 50 percent of your Social Security benefits.

If your combined income as a single filer exceeds $25,000 or as a married joint-filer exceeds the $32,000 income threshold, you may owe federal income tax up to 50 percent of your benefit. For combined incomes of $32,000 (single) or $44,000 (married), you are taxed up to 85 percent of your Social Security benefits.

The 85/15 percent payout theory is, like most pension and retirement plans that you contribute to, the IRS gives you credit for 15 percent as your contribution into the insurance plan and 85 percent as the growth portion.

Federal Insurance Contributions Act (FICA) tax is the US federal payroll or employment tax imposed on both employees and employers to fund our country's entitlement programs providing benefits for retirees, the disabled, and the children of deceased workers.

For 2015 and 2016, the SSA announced the maximum earnings subject to the 6.2% FICA tax is $118,500. Employers match the other 6.2%. The maximum SS tax is $7,347 for employees and employers. If you are self-employed, the same cap applies to the combined 12.4% self-employment tax.

For Medicare, add another 2.9% for that portion of FICA. The total self-employment tax rate is 15.3%. For employees, it is split between the employee and employer at 1.45/1.45%. If you make over $200,000 there is an additional .9% Medicare tax that only the worker is contributing with no cap.

This has caused some to claim that the payroll tax is not a tax because its collection is tied to a received benefit. It is more of a forced contribution to a collective, social system where we all hope—if needed—will receive a benefit from in the future. There goes the argument for our system being a double taxed system—meaning taxed on the income through payroll in the early years and taxed again on the SS retirement income. Do not be surprised, though, if the IRS or Congress decides to progress toward making SS income 100 percent taxable at a higher threshold or bracket in the future. Also, they can raise more revenue by raising the maximum earnings cap above $118,500 to higher levels or eliminating it, like the Medicare portion of FICA.

DID YOU KNOW?

Some states tax Social Security benefits, whereas other states may exempt them from taxation. This does make a difference on where some retirees decide to make their home in their retirement years.

In order to avoid a mistake resulting in current taxes and penalties, it is important to have a good understanding of retirement plan distribution methods and rules. Again, this is where a great financial advisor and tax advisor can make a big difference in your retirement income strategy.

In addition, there are experienced, independent insurance agents and financial professionals who focus on tax-deferred, safe money strategies that utilize guarantees of insurance companies.

Make sure to ask your advisor about tax-free strategies as well. The biggest regret I hear from my retired clients is that they did not set up enough (or any) tax-free retirement income types of accounts or investments. Even if you do not qualify for a Roth IRA, you still have options for tax-free retirement money.

If you plan properly you can have an even larger portion of your retirement dollars that fall into the tax-free income column.

CHAPTER 13

WOMEN AND SOCIAL SECURITY

So let's just admit it up front: Women are amazing! Without them there would be no us... not that men aren't integral in that formula, but they are not able to sustain life or give birth. Women wear multiple hats and play many roles throughout their lifetime, heck, throughout a single day! This chapter is not to elevate women to some higher level or put them on a pedestal, but merely to acknowledge that their role in our culture is uniquely different than men and ever changing.

More women in the 21st century than any other time in our nation's history work, pay Social Security taxes and earn credits towards their monthly benefit. Even with that reality, women are less often covered by private retirement accounts than men, making Social Security a key component to their retirement plan.

Women tend to receive Social Security benefits for a longer period of time than men for one obvious reason – they live longer than men. Historically, women outlive men by four to eight years. Today's life expectancy tables are closing the gap between men and women. On average, a man reaching age 65 can expect to live until age 84.3 and women to age 86.6. Even though we are all living longer and healthier lives, women in our culture still lean on Social Security for a larger portion of their income in retirement.

The number one issue affecting women's outlook on retirement is lack of adequate funds. Three in ten female beneficiaries, age 65 and older, rely almost solely on Social Security as their main income source. The average benefit for women 65 and older is approximately $13,500 per year, as compared to the average benefit for a male 65 and older, which is $17,600 per year. In light of those statistics the size of the survivor benefit suddenly becomes very important. The strategy and timing each spouse selects when filing for their Social Security benefit can drastically affect the size of that check each month for the surviving spouse.

Over the years, Social Security has adjusted and changed to meet the changing needs of women in America. The amount of benefits for the surviving spouse was increased. Financial protection for divorced women was improved by changing the number of years the couple must be married in order for the divorced spouse to qualify for benefits and a few other little tweaks.

The original purpose of Social Security was to take care of those Americans who lived exceptionally long lives or had disabilities leaving them in need of financial aid. It makes sense that changes are made periodically to keep up with the ever-changing landscape of our society.

Divorced spouses have become an unprotected portion of our population and need to be educated on the Social Security filing options that may still be available to them. If you are divorced but your marriage lasted 10 years or longer, you can receive benefits on your ex-spouse's Social Security record.

The qualifying factors are: You are unmarried, age 62 or older, your ex-spouse qualifies for a benefit and the benefit you personally are entitled to receive based on your own work is less than half the benefit you would receive based on your ex-spouse's record.

One major difference in the divorced filing strategy versus the traditional spousal filing strategy is your ex-spouse does not have to have filed for their benefit in order for you to receive benefits on his/her record. Imagine, if you will, that you went through a rather "messy" divorce. Lawyers' fees were racked up as every last asset was split and divvied up, your home was sold, your children uprooted and you tolerated the other at weddings and funerals only for the sake of the bride and groom or deceased. Imagine also that you had an opportunity to avenge yourself slightly by not electing for your benefit, knowing it would remove the option for your ex-spouse to file for a benefit based on your record.

One might be persuaded to hold off as long as possible just to spite the other. In order to protect each spouse from any possible power plays such as this one, Social Security allows you to file for a benefit based on your ex-spouse's record just as soon as he/her is eligible, which is 62 years old.

From another perspective: The new wife, a significantly younger woman who now finds herself sleeping beside your ex-husband is going to need a spousal benefit when she *finally* reaches her full retirement age. How has Social Security made provisions for her? She too, is eligible for a benefit based on her husband's record. Yes, you read that correctly—one work record on one man can be used for two (or more) separate spousal benefits at the same time.

Is it any wonder we seem to be spending down our Social Security faster than we are filling it up? That topic leads us right into the future of Social Security and we will get into that in a separate chapter. For now, recognize that these adjustments to our Social Security system were truly in the nature of protecting those in our culture who were left susceptible to financial hardship—divorcees are one such group.

To sum it all up, women are living longer and relying on Social Security statistically more than men and for a longer period of time. Couple that with the divorce factor and women are exposed to a higher risk of outliving their financial resources. Let's not forget the important role that women play in our retail economy as well. No woman wants to end up a bag lady, unless that bag is from Nordstrom's department store!

CHAPTER 14

SOCIAL SECURITY AND YOUR FUTURE

Imagine it is now the year 2033. You're in your 70s, well into your retirement years—enjoying the grandkids, traveling and planning a cruise to Alaska this summer, taking dance classes with your spouse once a week, volunteering in your community, and you have time to do what you want, when you want. Your monthly cash flow allows you to not only play and create memories, but to afford good health care coverage, quality foods, a safe car, a comfortable home, and to cover your living expenses. That $2,109 monthly check you receive from Social Security, after using some of our techniques you learned in the Social Security Success Guide, is the difference between just having a standard living, where you are just covering your living expenses, to now being able to sustain the quality life you worked so hard to enjoy. Your personal economy is strong and you are contributing to your local and national economy.

Then the US Government announces it is now 100 trillion dollars in debt. Congress can no longer, "kick that can down the road". They announce a plan to cut Social Security benefits, raise tax rates across the board, cut Medicare coverage and increase Part B premiums even more...yet again! Continued printing of the dollar by the Federal Reserve just to pay the interest on our national debt has caused above average inflation and prices of essential consumer goods are more than double, in some cases triple, where they are today.

I am not one to preach doom and gloom or argue from one political side or the other. What we have facing us currently and in the years to come is a math problem. Plain and simple. Well, maybe a lot of economics lessons mixed in too.

Current future unfunded liabilities are hovering close to 100 trillion. Of that, SS makes up $14.5 trillion and Medicare makes up $27.5 trillion. All of this is based on US Treasury numbers and statistical projections, which are aggregated on the site USDebtClock.org in a giant debt counter.

Here are some of the questions we need to be asking ourselves:

- Are you prepared to have the cost of food, clothes, gas, housing expenses, labor, and energy triple over the next 20 years?
- What do you want to happen if your retirement accounts don't grow to keep pace with inflation?
- What do you want to happen if your income doesn't keep up with your expenses?
- Will your insurance coverage keep up with your needed care and protection?
- Have you diversified how your income is taxed as well as what it is invested in?
- Do you think it makes sense to have some income sources that are tax-free?
- What do you want to happen if we experience a market crash a year or two before you want to retire?

- Are your assets and incomes sources protected should we have another event like 9/11?
- What areas in your life are you willing to cut back on if you see your assets starting to decrease and your incomes are not keeping pace with inflation or your expenses?

The reality is, what you need to prepare for and take responsibility for is—YOUR FURTURE. If things turn out great in your perfect little bubbles you live in, great! Everything you planned for is a bonus and you will have money left over for the kids, and grandchildren, and possibly your favorite charity after you are gone.

Here are some of the "golden nuggets" from the book that can help you thrive in your future and make sure Social Security survives:

- Social Security is designed to be inflation proof
- Great things come to those who wait to take their Social Security

- Social Security has (or had) several filing strategies to choose from to fit into your retirement plan
- Many filing strategies for under age 66 are going away at the end of April 2016.
- Take the time to learn how to apply these strategies to your family's personal economy
- Hire a competent retirement expert who knows how Social Security fits into your own personal economy
- Get involved and stay informed about political issues affecting you and our fellow Americans or our entitlements will be lowered

I've come to the conclusion after researching, writing this book, having been involved with actual cases, client scenarios and stories, that our Social Security system is part of what makes this country great. It is truly one of the finest financial plans that we have access to as hard working American citizens. If we are to survive and thrive with Social Security as a key piece of our retirement, we have to make sure the Social Security system survives!

We need to actively engage in retirement focused associations and political action groups. It is our duty to make sure we have this entitlement intact and sustainable for our future and families' futures for generations to come. By using our rights as Americans to stay informed of the issues and problems facing us, get involved in the community and vote. I challenge you to find a more well-rounded, benefit-packed investment or financial vehicle that we are guaranteed and entitled to receive from our country, The USA.

I'm glad you have bought this book. It is now one of your guides to making more income in your future. And most importantly, now you will have the knowledge and know-how to apply these strategies to increase your monthly income guaranteed to you by Uncle Sam. Wasn't it remarkable how little on this subject was told to us on how to do this—legally and guaranteed by our own government? Congratulations on joining us and helping spread these secrets and proven tactics to your loved ones. I invite you to join our community.

Join in and add to the discussion at:

www.SocialSecuritySuccess.Guide

or

www.facebook.com/gardenfinancial

Check for relevant articles on our blog at:

www.GardenFinance.com

If you have any questions, need to talk to someone regarding your Social Security and retirement, or for any potential speaking engagements on Social Security, Medicare or retirement related subjects contact:

Charlie Stivers at: cgstivers@gmail.com
Christy Sparks at: christyl.sparks@gmail.com

CHAPTER 15

SOURCES AND RESOURCES

The Social Security Administration maintains a website on the Internet, www.socialsecurity.gov or www.ssa.gov, where you can access and verify the preceding and even more information. It is considered public domain and it is where most of the information we have access to is located, but most don't know where to find it.

We are also providing you with the enclosed links that will help you with your research.

- Information for Financial Planners:
http://www.socialsecurity.gov/thirdparty/financial-planners.html

- Suspending Retirement Benefit Payments:
http://www.socialsecurity.gov/planners/retire/suspend.html

- Research, Statistics & Policy Analysis
http://www.socialsecurity.gov/policy/

- Solvency
http://www.socialsecurity.gov/oact/

- Trustees Report
http://www.socialsecurity.gov/oact/TR/2015/index.html

- FAQs
https://faq.ssa.gov/ics/support/default.asp?deptID=34019&_referrer=

- Publications
http://ssa.gov/pubs/

- Campaign for a Secure Retirement
http://ssa.gov/thirdparty/secureretirement/index.html

- Web Graphics and Banners
http://www.socialsecurity.gov/thirdparty/webgraphics.html

- Withdrawing application:
http://www.socialsecurity.gov/planners/retire/withdrawal.html

- Restricting the Scope of the Application:
http://www.socialsecurity.gov/planners/retire/applying6.html#&a0=1

- Retirement Data
http://www.socialsecurity.gov/policy/research_sub75.html

- US Summary of Assets and Liabilities
www.usdebtclock.org

NOTES & ACTION ITEMS:

Made in the USA
Middletown, DE
27 July 2016